Franklin D. Roosevelt

by Grace Hansen

ABDO
UNITED STATES
PRESIDENT BIOGRAPHIES
Kids

www.abdopublishing.com

Published by Abdo Kids, a division of ABDO, PO Box 398166, Minneapolis, Minnesota 55439.

Copyright © 2015 by Abdo Consulting Group, Inc. International copyrights reserved in all countries.
No part of this book may be reproduced in any form without written permission from the publisher.

Printed in the United States of America, North Mankato, Minnesota.

052014

092014

 THIS BOOK CONTAINS
RECYCLED MATERIALS

Photo Credits: Corbis, Getty Images, Shutterstock, Thinkstock

Production Contributors: Teddy Borth, Jennie Forsberg, Grace Hansen

Design Contributors: Candice Keimig, Laura Rask, Dorothy Toth

Library of Congress Control Number: 2013953006

Cataloging-in-Publication Data

Hansen, Grace.

 Franklin D. Roosevelt / Grace Hansen.

   p. cm. -- (United States president biographies)

ISBN 978-1-62970-088-5 (lib. bdg.)

Includes bibliographical references and index.

1. Roosevelt, Franklin D. (Franklin Delano), 1882-1945--Juvenile literature. 2. Presidents--United
States--Biography--Juvenile literature. I. Title.

973.917--dc23

[B]   2013953006

Table of Contents

Early Life

Franklin D. Roosevelt was born on January 30, 1882. He was born in Hyde Park, New York.

New York

Roosevelt had a happy childhood. He had a good education. He went to college and law school.

7

Family

Roosevelt married a

woman named Eleanor.

They had six children.

9

Becoming President

Roosevelt was a **lawyer**.
But he saw bigger things
in his future. He became
a New York state **senator**.

Roosevelt learned he had **polio**.

He was unable to walk. Eleanor

told him to carry on in politics.

13

Roosevelt did not give up.

In 1928, he ran for **governor**

of New York. He won.

Presidency

On March 4, 1933, Roosevelt

became the 32nd US president.

He helped the country through

the **Great Depression**.

Roosevelt then led the country through **World War II**. He helped create the **United Nations**. He wanted peace for all countries.

19

Death

On April 12, 1945, Roosevelt died. The American people were very sad. He cared for them in their hardest times.

21

More Facts

- One of Roosevelt's hobbies was stamp collecting. By the time of his death, his collection had over 1,200,000 stamps.

- One of the most famous first family pets is Fala, a Scottish terrier. Fala was Roosevelt's constant companion.

- Roosevelt served 4,422 days in office. That is 4 years longer than the next longest presidential term.

Glossary

governor – a person elected to be the head of a state in the US.

Great Depression – the period from 1929 to 1942 of worldwide economic trouble. Many people could not find work.

lawyer – a person who gives people advice on laws or represents them in court.

polio – the common name for poliomyelitis, which sometimes leaves people paralyzed.

senator – state senators are elected by districts within their home states. They represent their districts when voting.

United Nations (UN) – a group of nations formed in 1945. Its goals are peace, human rights, security, and social and economic development.

World War II – a war fought in Europe, Asia, and Africa from 1939 to 1945.

23

Index

abdokids.com

Use this code to log on to abdokids.com and access crafts, games, videos and more!

Abdo Kids Code:
UFK0885